MORE HYMNS
FOR TODAY

MORE HYMNS FOR TODAY

A SECOND SUPPLEMENT TO
Hymns Ancient and Modern

PRINTED FOR THE PROPRIETORS BY
WILLIAM CLOWES & SONS, LIMITED

Cover design by John Piper

FULL SCORE EDITION

First Published 1980

SET IN GREAT BRITAIN BY WILLIAM CLOWES & SONS LTD.,
LONDON AND GT. YARMOUTH.
PRINTED AND BOUND IN GREAT BRITAIN BY SPOTTISWOODE BALLANTYNE LTD.,
LONDON AND COLCHESTER.

PREFACE

Hymns are in origin popular religious songs belonging to a domestic and individual devotion before they find their way to supplementing the corporate liturgical worship of the Church. Even today they retain a more exploratory and unofficial character than we expect in a liturgy approved for general use. In both Catholic and Reformed traditions modern developments have sought to emphasise the active rather than the passive role of the people of God in the action of the liturgy, and good hymns help to realise this purpose.

In 1969 *100 Hymns for Today* appeared as a supplement to *Hymns Ancient and Modern*. This supplement has become so generally used in English-speaking churches that its capacity to meet contemporary need has been evident. Since 1969 there has been an unexpected, fresh, and exciting output of English hymns, which that supplement may have done something to bring about. Naturally enough, many of these new hymns are and have been intended by their authors to be experimental, written to help with an immediate task and with no ambition of bidding for permanent acceptance. The spiritual gift of writing the words of a great hymn is given to almost as few as the charism of composing good liturgical prose. But among these recent hymns there are those that have about them something of the elusive quality which seems to mark them with a more enduring character. At least they deserve to be tested for a longer time and introduced more widely in the service of the Church. Accordingly the editors now offer this second anthology. The intention is again double: to fill a few further gaps in *Hymns Ancient and Modern Revised* (1950) and to draw the best from the rich store of material generated since 1969. So Isaac Watts, Charles Wesley, and Athelstan Riley are here together with many writers of the late twentieth century.

It follows that this new supplement is intended not to be a substitute for *100 Hymns for Today* or *Hymns Ancient and Modern Revised*, but to be used alongside them and to enrich them. Like its predecessor the book seeks to be forward looking without abandoning ordered restraint; to be sensitive to the changing needs and renewed vitality of the Church in a turbulent world, while being rooted in the long, living tradition of the people of God.

Special mention must be made of Dr. Gerald H. Knight who, until his death in September 1979, was one of the editors, and served with distinction during his long and close association with *Hymns Ancient and Modern*.

June 1980

JOHN DYKES BOWER
EDGAR BISHOP
CYRIL TAYLOR
HENRY CHADWICK
LIONEL DAKERS

ACKNOWLEDGEMENTS

The Directors of Hymns Ancient & Modern Ltd thank the owners or controllers of copyright for permission to use the hymns and tunes listed below.

WORDS

AUTHOR	PERMISSION GRANTED BY	NO. OF HYMN
Alington, C. A.	Lady Mynors	159
Bayly, A. F.	Author	160, 161
Benson, L. F.	Cannot trace copyright owner	123
Bowers, J. E.	Author	111, 112, 113, 114, 129, 180
„	Free Church Choir Union	146
Bridge, B. E.	Author	133, 142
Briggs, G. W.	Oxford University Press	136
Clare, T. C. H.	Author	171
Cosnett, Elizabeth	Author	105
Crum, J. M. C.	Oxford University Press (from *The Oxford Book of Carols*)	168
Dobbie, R.	Author	119
Dudley-Smith, Timothy	Author	120
Foley, B.	Faber Music Ltd (from *New Catholic Hymnal*)	138, 152, 198
Franzmann, Martin	Concordia Publishing House	141
Fraser, I. M.	Stainer & Bell Ltd (from *New Songs for the Church*)	117
Gaunt, Alan	John Paul, the Preacher's Press	154
Gaunt, H. C. A.	Author	143, 162, 176
Green, F. Pratt	Oxford University Press	101, 107, 124, 145, 151 170, 175, 184, 191, 193
„	Stainer & Bell Ltd (from *Partners in Praise*)	131
Greenwood, H.	The Society of the Sacred Mission	185
Gregory, J. K.	Author	118
"Icarus, Peter"	Mayhew-McCrimmon Ltd, Great Wakering, Essex	174
Kaan, F.	Agape, Carol Stream, Il.60187, USA	148
„	B. Feldman & Co. Ltd, 138–140 Charing Cross Rd, London, WC2H oLD	189
„	Stainer & Bell Ltd (from *Partners in Praise*)	135, 167
Martin, Marcella	Stanbrook Abbey	155
Micklem, C.	Author	121
Oakley, C. E.	Oxford University Press (from *English Praise*)	137
O'Driscoll, T. H.	Author	134, 196
O'Neill, Judith	Author	188
Preston, G.	Novello & Co. Ltd	195
Quinn, J.	Geoffrey Chapman, a division of Cassell Ltd	125, 132, 183
Rees, T.	Community of the Resurrection	106
Riley, Athelstan	Oxford University Press (from *The English Hymnal*)	199
Riley, H.	Author	130
Routley, E.	Agape, Carol Stream, Il.60187, USA	165

An asterisk placed before the number of a verse indicates that the verse may be omitted, if so desired. An asterisk placed after an authors' name denotes some alteration of the original words.

The hymns are arranged alphabetically.

101 Folksong 9 8.9 8.

English Traditional Melody
arr. John Wilson

Organ Introduction to Verses 1 and 4

(mp)

senza Ped.

Voices in Unison

Ped. ad lib.

If any of Verses 1 to 3 are sung by the Choir alone, they may be in Harmony, with A.T.B. humming or singing a vowel sound; but Verse 4 should always be in Unison.

An Upper Room

Organ introduction

An upper room did our Lord prepare
   for those he loved until the end:
and his disciples still gather there,
   to celebrate their risen friend.

2

A lasting gift Jesus gave his own –
   to share his bread, his loving cup.
Whatever burdens may bow us down,
   he by his cross shall lift us up.

3

And after supper he washed their feet,
   for service, too, is sacrament.
In him our joy shall be made complete –
   sent out to serve, as he was sent.

Organ introduction

4

No end there is: we depart in peace.
   He loves beyond our uttermost:
in every room in our Father's house
   he will be there, as Lord and host.

F. PRATT GREEN (b. 1903)

The words were written for this tune

18th c. English Carol Melody

Unison

Refrain

Al - le - -lu - ya to Je - sus who died on the tree, and has raised up a lad - der of mer - cy for me, and has raised up a lad - der of mer - cy for me.

Jacob's Ladder

As Jacob with travel was weary one day,
at night on a stone for a pillow he lay;
he saw in a vision a ladder so high
that its foot was on earth and its top in the sky:

Alleluya to Jesus who died on the tree,
and has raised up a ladder of mercy for me.

2

This ladder is long, it is strong and well-made,
has stood hundreds of years and is not yet decayed;
many millions have climbed it and reached Sion's hill,
and thousands by faith are climbing it still:

3

Come let us ascend! all may climb it who will;
for the angels of Jacob are guarding it still:
and remember, each step that by faith we pass o'er,
some prophet or martyr has trod it before:

4

And when we arrive at the haven of rest
we shall hear the glad words, 'Come up hither, ye blest,
'here are regions of light, here are mansions of bliss'.
O who would not climb such a ladder as this?

Alleluya to Jesus who died on the tree,
and has raised up a ladder of mercy for me.

18th cent.

103 St. Petersburg   L.M.

Melody by D. S. Bortnianski (1752–1825)

The Christian Race

Awake, our souls; away, our fears;
   let every trembling thought be gone;
awake and run the heavenly race,
   and put a cheerful courage on.

2

True, 'tis a strait and thorny road,
   and mortal spirits tire and faint;
but they forget the mighty God
   that feeds the strength of every saint:

3

the mighty God, whose matchless power
   is ever new and ever young,
and firm endures, while endless years
   their everlasting circles run.

4

From thee, the overflowing spring,
   our souls shall drink a fresh supply,
while such as trust their native strength
   shall melt away, and drop, and die.

5

Swift as an eagle cuts the air,
   we'll mount aloft to thine abode;
on wings of love our souls shall fly,
   nor tire amidst the heavenly road.

ISAAC WATTS (1674–1748)
Isaiah 40. 28–31

104 Blairgowrie 8 8.8 6.8 6.   R. G. Thompson (1862–1934)

Al - le - lu – ia, al - le -

lu – ia,

A new spring

Away with gloom, away with doubt,
  with all the morning stars we sing;
with all the sons of God we shout
  the praises of a King,
    Alleluia, alleluia,
  of our returning King.

2

Away with death, and welcome life;
  in him we died and live again:
and welcome peace, away with strife,
  for he returns to reign.
    Alleluia, alleluia,
  the Crucified shall reign.

3

Then welcome beauty, he is fair;
  and welcome youth, for he is young;
and welcome spring; and everywhere
  let merry songs be sung,
    Alleluia, alleluia,
  for such a King be sung.

EDWARD SHILLITO (1872–1948)

105 Epworth C.M.

Adapted from a melody by Charles Wesley the younger (1757–1834) based on the harmonisation by Martin Shaw (1875–1958)

Alternative Tune: *St. Bernard* (A.M.R. 104; E.H. 71; S.P. 537)

The Light of Christ

1

Can man by searching find out God
  or formulate his ways?
can numbers measure what he is
  or words contain his praise?

2

Although his being is too bright
  for human eyes to scan,
his meaning lights our shadowed world
  through Christ, the Son of Man.

3

Our boastfulness is turned to shame,
  our profit counts as loss,
when earthly values stand beside
  the manger and the cross.

4

We there may recognise his light,
  may kindle in its rays,
find there the source of penitence,
  the starting-point for praise.

5

There God breaks in upon our search,
  makes birth and death his own:
he speaks to us in human terms
  to make his glory known.

ELIZABETH COSNETT (b. 1936)

The Body of Christ

Christ is the heavenly food that gives
   to every famished soul
new life and strength, new joy and hope,
   and faith to make them whole.

2

We all are made for God alone,
   without him we are dead;
no food suffices for the soul,
   but Christ, the living bread.

3

Christ is the unity that binds
   in one the near and far;
for we who share his life divine
   his living body are.

4

On earth and in the realms beyond
   one fellowship are we;
and at his altar we are knit
   in mystic unity.

TIMOTHY REES (1874–1939)

Christe sanctorum   10 11 11.6.   Melody from *Paris Antiphoner, 1681*

Unison

No other Name

Christ is the world's light, he and none other:
born in our darkness, he became our brother;
if we have seen him, we have seen the Father:
    Glory to God on high.

2

Christ is the world's peace, he and none other:
no man can serve him and despise his brother;
who else unites us, one in God the Father?
    Glory to God on high.

3

Christ is the world's life, he and none other;
sold once for silver, murdered here, our brother –
he, who redeems us, reigns with God the Father:
    Glory to God on high.

4

Give God the glory, God and none other;
give God the glory, Spirit, Son and Father;
give God the glory, God in man my brother;
    Glory to God on high.

F. PRATT GREEN (b. 1903)

108 Feniton 7 8.7 8. and Alleluias Sydney H. Nicholson (1875–1947)

Al - le - lu - ia, Al - le - lu - ia, Al - le - lu - ia.

Voices

Organ

No Ped.

Ped.

Transfiguration

Christ upon the mountain peak
  stands alone in glory blazing;
let us, if we dare to speak,
  with the saints and angels praise him:
      Alleluia.

2

Trembling at his feet we saw
  Moses and Elijah speaking;
all the prophets and the Law
  shout through them their joyful greeting:
      Alleluia.

3

Swift the cloud of glory came,
  God proclaiming in the thunder
Jesus as his Son by name;
  nations, cry aloud in wonder!
      Alleluia.

4

This is God's belovèd Son:
  Law and prophets fade before him;
First and Last, and only One,
  let creation now adore him.
      Alleluia.

BRIAN A. WREN (b. 1936)

109 Caithness C.M.

The Baptism of Jesus

Christ, when for us you were baptized
    God's Spirit on you came,
as peaceful as a dove, and yet
    as urgent as a flame.

2

God called you his belovèd Son,
    called you his servant too;
his kingdom you were called to preach,
    his holy will to do.

3

Straightway and steadfast until death
    you then obeyed his call,
freely as Son of Man to serve,
    and give your life for all.

4

Baptize us with your Spirit, Lord,
    your cross on us be signed,
that likewise in God's service we
    may perfect freedom find.

F. BLAND TUCKER (b. 1895)

Ave virgo virginum 7 6.7 6.D.

Melody as given by
J. Horn (1544)

New Life

Christian people, raise your song,
    chase away all grieving;
sing your joy and be made strong,
    our Lord's life receiving;
nature's gifts of wheat and vine
    now are set before us:
as we offer bread and wine
    Christ comes to restore us.

2

Come to welcome Christ today,
    God's great revelation;
he has pioneered the way
    of the new creation.
Greet him, Christ our risen King
    gladly recognizing,
as with joy men greet the spring
    out of winter rising.

COLIN P. THOMPSON (b. 1945)

111 Salve festa dies
Irregular
R. Vaughan Williams (1872–1958)

Verse 1 (repeated as a refrain after verses 2 to 7)

Chris - tians, lift up your hearts, and make this a day of re - joic - ing; God is our strength and song: glo - ry and praise to his name!

Verses 2, 4, 6

2. Praise for the Spi - rit of God, who _
*4. Praise that his love ov - er - flowed in the
6. Come, Ho - ly Spi - rit, to us, who _

came to the wait - ing dis - ci - ples; there in the _
hearts of _ all who re - ceived him, join - ing to -
live by your pre - sence with - in us, come to di -

wind and the fire _ God gave new life to his own:
geth - er in peace _ those once di - vid - ed by sin:
rect our _ course, give us your life and your power:

Repeat refrain

Verses 3, 5 and 7 overleaf

111 *(continued)*

Verses 3, 5, 7

3. God's migh-ty power was re - vealed when those who
*5. Strength-ened by God's migh-ty power the dis - ci - ples went
7. Spi - rit of God, send us out to live to your

once were so fear - ful now could be seen by the
out to all na - tions, preach-ing the gos-pel of
praise and your glo - ry; yours is the power and the

world wit - ness-ing brave - ly for Christ:
Christ, laugh - ing at dan - ger and death:
might, ours be the cour - age and faith:

Repeat refrain

Praise for the Spirit

Christians, lift up your hearts, and make this a day of rejoicing;
God is our strength and song: glory and praise to his name!

2

Praise for the Spirit of God, who came to the waiting disciples;
there in the wind and the fire God gave new life to his own:

3

God's mighty power was revealed when those who once were so fearful
now could be seen by the world witnessing bravely for Christ:

*4

Praise that his love overflowed in the hearts of all who received him,
joining together in peace those once divided by sin:

*5

Strengthened by God's mighty power the disciples went out to all nations,
preaching the gospel of Christ, laughing at danger and death:

6

Come, Holy Spirit, to us, who live by your presence within us,
come to direct our course, give us your life and your power:

7

Spirit of God, send us out to live to your praise and your glory;
yours is the power and the might, ours be the courage and faith:

Christians, lift up your hearts, and make this a day of rejoicing;
God is our strength and song: glory and praise to his name!

JOHN E. BOWERS (b. 1923)

112 Salve festa dies   R. Vaughan Williams (1872–1958)
Irregular

Verse 1 (repeated as a refrain after verses 2 to 7)

Chris - tians, lift up your hearts, and make this a day of re - joic - ing; God is our strength and song; glo - ry and praise to his name!

Verses 2, 4, 6

2. This is the house of the Lord, where
4. Here God's life- giv - ing word once
6. Sum-moned by Christ's com - mand his

seek - ers and find - ers are wel - come; en - ter its__
more is pro-claimed to his peo - ple, up - lift - ing__
peo - ple draw near to his ta - ble, glad - ly to__

gates with your praise, fill all its courts with your song:
those who are down, chal - leng-ing all with its truth:
greet their Lord, known in the break - ing of bread:

Repeat refrain

Verses 3, 5 and 7 overleaf

Verses 3, 5, 7

3. All those bap-tized in - to Christ share the glo - ry of
5. Those who are bur-dened with sin find__ here the__
7. Strong and a - lert in his grace, God's peo - ple are

his re - sur - rec - tion, dy - ing with him un - to
joy of for - give - ness, lay - ing their sins be - fore
one in their wor - ship; kept by his peace they de-

sin, walk - ing in new - ness of life:____
Christ, par - don and peace their re - ward:____
part, rea - dy for ser - ving their Lord:____

Repeat refrain

The House of God

Christians, lift up your hearts, and make this a day of rejoicing;
  God is our strength and song; glory and praise to his name!

2

This is the house of the Lord, where seekers and finders are welcome;
  enter its gates with your praise, fill all its courts with your song:

3

All those baptized into Christ share the glory of his resurrection,
  dying with him unto sin, walking in newness of life:

4

Here God's life-giving word once more is proclaimed to his people,
  uplifting those who are down, challenging all with its truth:

5

Those who are burdened with sin find here the joy of forgiveness,
  laying their sins before Christ, pardon and peace their reward:

6

Summoned by Christ's command his people draw near to his table,
  gladly to greet their Lord, known in the breaking of bread:

7

Strong and alert in his grace, God's people are one in their worship;
  kept by his peace they depart, ready for serving their Lord:

Christians, lift up your hearts, and make this a day of rejoicing;
  God is our strength and song; glory and praise to his name!

JOHN E. BOWERS (b. 1923)

113 Salve festa dies   R. Vaughan Williams (1872–1958)

Irregular

Verse 1 (repeated as a refrain after verses 2 and 3)

Chris - tians, lift up your hearts, and

make this a day of re - joic - ing; God is our strength and

song: glo - ry and praise to his name!

Verse 2

Here God's life - giv - ing word once

more is pro-claimed to his peo - ple, up - lift - ing

those who are down, chal - leng-ing all with its truth:

Repeat refrain

Verse 3 overleaf

113 (continued)

Verse 3

Sum-moned by Christ's com - mand his— peo - ple draw
near to his ta - ble, glad-ly to greet— their
Lord, known in the break - ing of bread:—

Repeat refrain

Word and Sacrament

Christians, lift up your hearts, and make this a day of rejoicing;
God is our strength and song: glory and praise to his name!

2

Here God's life-giving word once more is proclaimed to his people,
uplifting those who are down, challenging all with its truth:

3

Summoned by Christ's command his people draw near to his table,
gladly to greet their Lord, known in the breaking of bread:

Christians, lift up your hearts, and make this a day of rejoicing;
God is our strength and song: glory and praise to his name!

John E. Bowers (b. 1923)

114 Alleluia, dulce carmen 8 7.8 7.8 7.
(Tantum ergo)

Melody from *An Essay on
the Church Plain Chant*, 1782

Offertory

Christians, lift your hearts and voices,
   let your praises be outpoured;
come with joy and exultation
   to the table of the Lord;
come believing, come expectant,
   in obedience to his word.

2

See, presiding at his table,
   Jesus Christ our great high priest;
where he summons all his people,
   none is greatest, none is least;
graciously he bids them welcome
   to the eucharistic feast.

3

Lord, we offer in thanksgiving
   life and work for you to bless;
yet unworthy is the offering,
   marred by pride and carelessness;
so, Lord, pardon our transgressions,
   plant in us true holiness.

4

On the evening of his passion
   Jesus gave the wine and bread,
so that all who love and serve him
   shall for evermore be fed.
Taste and see the Lord is gracious,
   feed upon the living bread.

JOHN E. BOWERS (b. 1923)

Melody from *Praxis pietatis melica*, 1647

Before reading the Scriptures

Come, Holy Ghost, our hearts inspire,
   let us thine influence prove;
source of the old prophetic fire,
   fountain of life and love.

2

Come, Holy Ghost – for, moved by thee,
   thy prophets wrote and spoke –
unlock the truth, thyself the key,
   unseal the sacred book.

3

Expand thy wings, celestial Dove,
   brood o'er our nature's night;
on our disordered spirits move,
   and let there now be light.

4

God, through himself, we then shall know,
   if thou within us shine;
and sound, with all thy saints below,
   the depths of love divine.

CHARLES WESLEY (1707–88)

The Lord's Day

Come, let us with our Lord arise,
our Lord who made both earth and skies,
   and gave men gifts of life and peace;
he died to save the world he made,
he rose triumphant from the dead,
   and stamped the day for ever his.

2

This is the day the Lord has made,
that all may see his power displayed,
   be filled with all the life of God;
may feel his resurrection's power,
and rise again, to fall no more,
   in perfect righteousness renewed.

3

Then let us render him his own,
with solemn prayer approach his throne,
   our joyful hearts and voices raise;
with meekness hear the gospel word,
with thanks his dying love record,
   and fill his courts with songs of praise.

CHARLES WESLEY* (1707–88)

117 England's Lane 7 7.7 7.7 7.

Adapted from an English melody
by Geoffrey Shaw (1879–1943)

Unison

Alternative Tune: *Heathlands* (A.M.R. 264; E.H. 395; S.P. 170)

At a Wedding

Crown with love, Lord, this glad day,
   love to humble and delight,
love which until death will stay,
   testing all life's depth and height;
such a love as took our part,
spendthrift in its generous art.

2

Lord, give joy on this glad day,
   joy to face life's hurt and ill,
all that tests the wedded way,
   forging union deeper still;
joy like his who, for our gain,
lightly weighed the cross and pain.

3

Crown with peace, Lord, this glad day,
   peace the world may not invent,
nor misfortune strip away
   from two hearts in you content,
knowing love will never cease
from that source who is our peace.

IAN M. FRASER (b. 1917)

118 St. Bavon 8 7.8 7.   A. T. I. Jagger (b. 1911)

When the tune is sung in harmony, in the last line the upper of the two tenor
parts may be used.

With us always

Early morning. 'Come, prepare him,
  to the tomb your spices bring;
death is cold and death decaying,
  we must beautify our King.'

2

Early morning, women excited,
  seeking Peter everywhere;
telling of a man who told them,
  'He is risen: don't despair'.

3

Peter racing, early morning,
  to the tomb and rushing in;
seeing shrouds of death dispensed with,
  finding new-born faith begin.

4

Early morning, Mary weeping,
  asking if the gardener knew;
knowing, as his voice says, 'Mary',
  'Lord, Rabbuni, it is you'.

5

'Mary, you can live without me,
  as I now to God ascend;
peace be with you; I am with you
  early morning without end.'

6

Early morning, stay for ever,
  early morning, never cease;
early morning, come to all men
  for their good and power and peace.

JOHN GREGORY (b. 1929)

119 St. Fulbert C.M.   H. J. Gauntlett (1805–76)

Baptized into Christ

Eternal God, we consecrate
  these children to your care,
to you their talents dedicate,
  for they your image bear.

2

To them our solemn pledge we give
  their lives by prayer to shield.
May they in truth and honour live,
  and to your guidance yield.

3

Your Spirit's power on them bestow,
  from sin their hearts preserve;
in Christ their master may they grow,
  and him for ever serve.

4

So may the waters of this rite
  become a means of grace,
and these your children show the light
  that shone in Jesus' face.

ROBERT DOBBIE (b. 1901)

Pastor pastorum 6 5.6 5.   F. Silcher (1789–1860)

Nunc Dimittis

Faithful vigil ended,
  watching, waiting cease;
Master, grant thy servant
  his discharge in peace.

2

All thy Spirit promised,
  all the Father willed,
now these eyes behold it
  perfectly fulfilled.

3

This thy great deliverance
  sets thy people free;
Christ their light uplifted
  all the nations see.

4

Christ, thy people's glory!
  Watching, doubting cease;
grant to us thy servants
  our discharge in peace.

TIMOTHY DUDLEY-SMITH (b. 1926)
Luke 2. 29–32 (N.E.B.)

All kinds of light   5.8 8.5 5.   Caryl Micklem (b. 1925)

Unison

All kinds of light

Father, we thank you
for the light that shines all the day;
  for the bright sky you have given,
  most like your heaven;
    Father, we thank you.

2

Father, we thank you
for the lamps that lighten the way;
  for human skill's exploration
  of your creation;
    Father, we thank you.

3

Father, we thank you
for the friends who brighten our play;
  for your command to call others
  sisters and brothers;
    Father, we thank you.

4

Father, we thank you
for your love in Jesus today,
  giving us hope for tomorrow
  through joy and sorrow;
    Father, we thank you.

CARYL MICKLEM (b. 1925)

122 Surrexit 8 8 8. and Alleluias   A. Gregory Murray (b. 1905)

Unison

Al - le - lu - ia, al - le - lu - ia!

Swallowed up in victory

Finished the strife of battle now,
gloriously crowned the victor's brow:
sing with gladness, hence with sadness:

Alleluia, alleluia!

2

After the death that him befell,
Jesus Christ has harrowed hell:
songs of praising we are raising:

3

On the third morning he arose,
shining with victory o'er his foes;
earth is singing, heaven is ringing:

4

Lord, by your wounds on you we call:
now that from death you've freed us all:
may our living be thanksgiving:

Alleluia, alleluia!

tr. J. M. NEALE* (1818–66)

123

FIRST TUNE

Wraysbury 8 7.8 7.   E. J. Hopkins (1818–1901)

SECOND TUNE

Omni die 8 7.8 7.

Melody from Corner's *Gesangbuch,* 1631
arr. W. S. Rockstro (1823–95)

After Communion

For the bread which you have broken,
    for the wine which you have poured,
for the words which you have spoken,
    now we give you thanks, O Lord.

2

By these pledges that you love us,
    by your gift of peace restored,
by your call to heaven above us,
    hallow all our lives, O Lord.

3

In your service, Lord, defend us,
    in our hearts keep watch and ward;
in the world to which you send us
    let your kingdom come, O Lord.

L. F. BENSON (1855–1930)

East Acklam   8 4.8 4.8 8 8.4.   Francis Jackson (b. 1917)

Harvest

For the fruits of his creation,
   thanks be to God;
for his gifts to every nation,
   thanks be to God;
for the ploughing, sowing, reaping,
silent growth while men are sleeping,
future needs in earth's safe keeping,
   thanks be to God.

2

In the just reward of labour,
   God's will is done;
in the help we give our neighbour,
   God's will is done;
in our world-wide task of caring
for the hungry and despairing,
in the harvests men are sharing,
   God's will is done.

3

For the harvests of his Spirit,
   thanks be to God;
for the good all men inherit,
   thanks be to God;
for the wonders that astound us,
for the truths that still confound us,
most of all, that love has found us,
   thanks be to God.

F. PRATT GREEN (b. 1903)

125 Duke Street   L.M.

Late 18th c. melody
attributed to J. Hatton (d. 1793)

Prophets, priests, and kings

Forth in the peace of Christ we go;
   Christ to the world with joy we bring;
Christ in our minds, Christ on our lips,
   Christ in our hearts, the world's true King.

2

King of our hearts, Christ makes us kings;
   kingship with him his servants gain;
with Christ, the Servant-Lord of all,
   Christ's world we serve to share Christ's reign.

3

Priests of the world, Christ sends us forth
   this world of time to consecrate,
this world of sin by grace to heal,
   Christ's world in Christ to re-create.

4

Christ's are our lips, his word we speak;
   prophets are we whose deeds proclaim
Christ's truth in love, that we may be
   Christ in the world, to spread Christ's name.

5

We are the Church; Christ bids us show
   that in his Church all nations find
their hearth and home, where Christ restores
   true peace, true love, to all mankind.

JAMES QUINN (b. 1919)

126 Sing Hosanna   10 8.10 9. and Refrain   Traditional Melody

Hosanna

Give me joy in my heart, keep me praising,
  give me joy in my heart, I pray;
give me joy in my heart, keep me praising,
  keep me praising till the break of day.

    Sing hosanna, sing hosanna,
    sing hosanna to the King of kings!
    Sing hosanna, sing hosanna,
    sing hosanna to the King!

2

Give me peace in my heart, keep me loving,
  give me peace in my heart, I pray;
give me peace in my heart, keep me loving,
  keep me loving till the break of day:

3

Give me love in my heart, keep me serving,
  give me love in my heart, I pray;
give me love in my heart, keep me serving,
  keep me serving till the break of day:

    Sing hosanna, sing hosanna,
    sing hosanna to the King of kings!
    Sing hosanna, sing hosanna,
    sing hosanna to the King!

Traditional

127 Dunedin L.M.   Vernon Griffiths (b. 1894)

Alternative Tune: *Warrington* (A.M.R. 153; E.H. 263; S.P. 25)

The Salvation of God

Give to our God immortal praise;
mercy and truth are all his ways:
    wonders of grace to God belong,
    repeat his mercies in your song.

2

Give to the Lord of lords renown,
the King of kings with glory crown:
    his mercies ever shall endure
    when lords and kings are known no more.

3

He sent his Son with power to save
from guilt and darkness and the grave:
    wonders of grace to God belong,
    repeat his mercies in your song.

4

Through this vain world he guides our feet,
and leads us to his heavenly seat:
    his mercies ever shall endure,
    when this vain world shall be no more.

ISAAC WATTS (1674–1748)
Psalm 136

128 Benifold 8.3 3.6.D. Francis B. Westbrook (1903–75)

Glory, love, and praise, and honour
    for our food
    now bestowed
  render we the Donor.
Bounteous God, we now confess thee;
    God, who thus
    blessest us,
  meet it is to bless thee.

2

Thankful for our every blessing,
    let us sing
    Christ the Spring,
  never, never ceasing.
Source of all our gifts and graces
    Christ we own;
    Christ alone
  calls for all our praises.

3

He dispels our sin and sadness,
    life imparts,
    cheers our hearts,
  fills with food and gladness.
Who himself for all hath given,
    us he feeds,
    us he leads
  to a feast in heaven.

CHARLES WESLEY (1707–88)

R. R. Terry (1865–1938)

Made Flesh

'Glory to God!' all heav'n with joy is ringing;
   angels proclaim the gospel of Christ's birth –
'Glory to God!', and still their song is bringing
   good news of God incarnate here on earth.

2

Lowly in wonder shepherds kneel before him,
   no gift to bring save love of heart and mind.
Come like those shepherds, sing his praise, adore him,
   a babe so weak, yet Saviour of mankind.

3

Humble, yet regal, wise men kneel before him,
   gold, incense, myrrh, their gifts to Christ they bring.
Come like those wise men, sing his praise, adore him,
   a babe so poor and modest, yet a King.

4

Though now no crib or cradle is concealing
   Jesus our Lord in that far-distant shrine,
Christ at each eucharist is still revealing
   his very self in forms of bread and wine.

JOHN E. BOWERS (b. 1923)

Lobet den Herren   11 11 11.5.   Melody by J. Crüger (1598–1662)

Unison or Harmony

To the altar of God

God everlasting, wonderful and holy,
Father most gracious, we who stand before thee
here at thine altar, as thy Son has taught us,
  come to adore thee.

2

Countless the mercies thou hast lavished on us,
source of all blessing to all creatures living,
to thee we render, for thy love o'erflowing,
  humble thanksgiving.

3

Now in remembrance of our great Redeemer,
dying on Calvary, rising and ascending,
through him we offer what he ever offers,
  sinners befriending.

4

Strength to the living, rest to the departed,
grant, Holy Father, through this pure oblation;
may the life-giving Bread for ever bring us
  health and salvation.

HAROLD RILEY (b. 1903)

131 Blaenwern 8 7.8 7.D. William P. Rowlands (1860–1937)

God is here; as we his people
   meet to offer praise and prayer,
may we find in fuller measure
   what it is in Christ we share.
Here, as in the world around us,
   all our varied skills and arts
wait the coming of his Spirit
   into open minds and hearts.

2

Here are symbols to remind us
   of our lifelong need of grace;
here are table, font and pulpit,
   here the cross has central place;
here in honesty of preaching,
   here in silence as in speech,
here in newness and renewal
   God the Spirit comes to each.

3

Here our children find a welcome
   in the Shepherd's flock and fold,
here, as bread and wine are taken,
   Christ sustains us, as of old.
Here the servants of the Servant
   seek in worship to explore
what it means in daily living
   to believe and to adore.

4

Lord of all, of Church and Kingdom,
   in an age of change and doubt
keep us faithful to the gospel,
   help us work your purpose out.
Here, in this day's dedication,
   all we have to give, receive.
We, who cannot live without you,
   we adore you, we believe.

F. PRATT GREEN (b. 1903)

132 Ubi caritas 12 12 12 12 and Refrain   A. Gregory Murray (b. 1905)

Refrain   Unison

God is love, and where true love is, , God him-self is there.

Verses (Choir harmony ad lib)

Unison Refrain

Serving Christ in one another

God is love, and where true love is, God himself is there.

Here in Christ we gather, love of Christ our calling.
Christ, our love, is with us, gladness be his greeting.
Let us all revere and love him, God eternal.
Loving him, let each love Christ in all his brothers.

God is love, and where true love is, God himself is there.

2

When we Christians gather, members of one Body,
let there be in us no discord, but one spirit.
Banished now be anger, strife and every quarrel.
Christ, our God, be present always here among us.

God is love, and where true love is, God himself is there.

3

Grant us love's fulfilment, joy with all the blessèd,
when we see your face, O Saviour, in its glory.
Shine on us, O purest Light of all creation,
be our bliss while endless ages sing your praises.

God is love, and where true love is, God himself is there.

From the Latin Liturgy of Maundy Thursday
tr. JAMES QUINN (b. 1919)

For another translation see no. 195

133   Oriel   8 7.8 7.8 7.

C. Ett's *Cantica Sacra*, 1840

Baptism

God the Father, name we treasure,
   each new generation draws
from the past that you have given
   for the future that is yours;
may these children, in your keeping,
   love your ways, obey your laws.

2

Christ, the name that Christians carry,
   Christ, who from the Father came,
calling men to share your sonship,
   for these children grace we claim;
may they be your true disciples,
   yours in deed as well as name.

3

Holy Spirit, from the Father
   on the friends of Jesus poured,
may our children share those graces
   promised to them in the Word,
and their gifts find rich fulfilment,
   dedicated to our Lord.

BASIL E. BRIDGE (b. 1927)

Causa divina   14 14.4 7.8.   Frederick R. C. Clarke (b. 1931)

Unison

'Read, mark, learn . . . '

God, who hast caused to be written thy word for our learning,
grant us that, hearing, our hearts may be inwardly burning.
  Give to us grace,
    that in thy Son we embrace
  life, all its glory discerning.

2

Now may our God give us joy, and his peace in believing
all things were written in truth for our thankful receiving.
  As Christ did preach
    from man to man love must reach,
  grant us each day love's achieving.

3

Lord, should the powers of the earth and the heavens be shaken,
grant us to see thee in all things, our vision awaken.
  Help us to see,
    though all the earth cease to be,
  thy truth shall never be shaken.

T. HERBERT O'DRISCOLL (b. 1928)

135 New Malden   8 7.8 7.8 7.

David McCarthy (b. 1931)

Alternative Tune: *Rhuddlan* (A.M.R. 556; E.H. 423; S.P. 552)

The first and final word

God who spoke in the beginning,
  forming rock and shaping spar,
set all life and growth in motion,
  earthly world and distant star;
he who calls the earth to order
  is the ground of what we are.

2

God who spoke through men and nations,
  through events long past and gone,
showing still today his purpose,
  speaks supremely through his Son;
he who calls the earth to order
  gives his word and it is done.

3

God whose speech becomes incarnate –
  Christ is servant, Christ is Lord –
calls us to a life of service,
  heart and will to action stirred;
he who uses man's obedience
  has the first and final word.

FRED KAAN (b. 1929)

136 Bangor C.M.   Melody from W. Tans'ur's *Compleat Melody*, 1735

Science

God, you have giv'n us power to sound
  depths hitherto unknown:
to probe earth's hidden mysteries,
  and make their might our own.

2

Great are your gifts: yet greater far
  this gift, O God, bestow,
that as to knowledge we attain
  we may in wisdom grow.

3

Let wisdom's godly fear dispel
  all fears that hate impart;
give understanding to the mind,
  and with new mind new heart.

4

So for your glory and our good
  may we your gifts employ,
lest, maddened by the lust of power,
  we shall ourselves destroy.

G. W. BRIGGS* (1875–1959)

137 Little Cornard 66.66.88. Martin Shaw (1875–1958)

Unison

Hope of the World

Hills of the North, rejoice,
  echoing songs arise,
hail with united voice
  him who made earth and skies:
he comes in righteousness and love,
he brings salvation from above.

2

Isles of the Southern seas,
  sing to the listening earth,
carry on every breeze
  hope of a world's new birth:
in Christ shall all be made anew,
his word is sure, his promise true.

3

Lands of the East, arise,
  he is your brightest morn,
greet him with joyous eyes,
  praise shall his path adorn:
the God whom you have longed to know
in Christ draws near, and calls you now.

4

Shores of the utmost West,
  lands of the setting sun,
welcome the heavenly guest
  in whom the dawn has come:
he brings a never-ending light
who triumphed o'er our darkest night.

5

Shout, as you journey on,
  songs be in every mouth,
lo, from the North they come,
  from East and West and South:
in Jesus all shall find their rest,
in him the sons of earth be blest.

Editors of English Praise
based on C. E. Oakley (1832–65)

138 All for Jesus   8 7.8 7.   John Stainer (1840–1901)

Life in the Spirit

Holy Spirit, come, confirm us
    in the truth that Christ makes known;
we have faith and understanding
    through your helping gifts alone.

2

Holy Spirit, come, console us,
    come as Advocate to plead,
loving Spirit from the Father,
    grant in Christ the help we need.

3

Holy Spirit, come, renew us,
    come yourself to make us live,
holy through your loving presence,
    holy through the gifts you give.

4

Holy Spirit, come, possess us,
    you the love of Three in One,
Holy Spirit of the Father,
    Holy Spirit of the Son.

BRIAN FOLEY (b. 1919)

Melody from Corner's
Geistliche Nachtigal, 1649
harm. John Wilson

The majesty of God

How shall I sing that majesty
    which angels do admire?
let dust in dust and silence lie;
    sing, sing, ye heavenly choir.
Thousands of thousands stand around
    thy throne, O God most high;
ten thousand times ten thousand sound
    thy praise; but who am I?

2

Thy brightness unto them appears,
    whilst I thy footsteps trace;
a sound of God comes to my ears,
    but they behold thy face.
They sing because thou art their Sun;
    Lord, send a beam on me;
for where heav'n is but once begun
    there alleluias be.

3

How great a being, Lord, is thine,
    which doth all beings keep!
Thy knowledge is the only line
    to sound so vast a deep.
Thou art a sea without a shore,
    a sun without a sphere;
thy time is now and evermore,
    thy place is everywhere.

JOHN MASON (*c.* 1645–1694)

St. Botolph   C.M.   Gordon Slater (1896–1979)

Christ making friends

I come with joy to meet my Lord,
   forgiven, loved, and free,
in awe and wonder to recall
   his life laid down for me.

2

I come with Christians far and near
   to find, as all are fed,
man's true community of love
   in Christ's communion bread.

3

As Christ breaks bread for men to share,
   each proud division ends.
The love that made us, makes us one,
   and strangers now are friends.

4

And thus with joy we meet our Lord.
   His presence, always near,
is in such friendship better known:
   we see, and praise him here.

5

Together met, together bound,
   we'll go our different ways,
and as his people in the world,
   we'll live and speak his praise.

BRIAN A. WREN (b. 1936)

141 St. Nicholas   C.M.   Melody from Holdroyd's *The Spiritual Man's Companion*, 1753, as adapted in *Scottish Psalmody*, 1854

Lost and found

In Adam we have all been one,
    one huge rebellious man;
we all have fled that evening voice
    that sought us as we ran.

2

We fled thee and, in losing thee,
    we lost our brother too;
each singly sought and claimed his own,
    each man his brother slew.

3

But thy strong love, it sought us still,
    and sent thine only Son
that we might hear his shepherd's voice
    and, hearing him, be one.

4

O thou who, when we loved thee not,
    didst love and save us all,
thou great Good Shepherd of mankind,
    O hear us when we call.

5

Send us thy Spirit, teach us truth;
    thou Son, O set us free
from fancied wisdom, self-sought ways,
    to make us one in thee.

MARTIN FRANZMANN (1907–1976)

142

Seelenbräutigam   5 5.8 8.5 5.   A. Drese (1620–1701)

SECOND TUNE

Westron Wynde   5 5.8 8.5 5.   William Llewellyn (b. 1925)

The first tune may be found more suitable for congregations, the second for choirs, e.g. while the Registers are signed.

At a Wedding

Jesus, Lord, we pray,
  be our guest today;
gospel story has recorded
how your glory was afforded
  to a wedding day;
  be our guest, we pray.

2

Lord of love and life,
  blessing man and wife,
as they stand, their need confessing,
may your hand take theirs in blessing;
  you will share their life;
  bless this man and wife.

3

Lord of hope and faith,
  faithful unto death,
let the ring serve as a token
of a love sincere, unbroken,
  love more strong than death;
  Lord of hope and faith.

BASIL E. BRIDGE (b. 1927)

143

Buriton 4 5.4 5.D. Cyril V. Taylor (b. 1907)

Best of all friends

1

Jesus, my Lord,
  let me be near you;
by your own word
  help me to hear you.
Jesus, my Lord,
  lead me to love you,
nothing more dear,
  no one above you.

2

All through the day,
  sisters and brothers,
yours we will be,
  caring for others,
hearing your words,
  learning your story,
bearing your cross,
  sharing your glory.

3

Teach us to know
  seeing from blindness,
help us to show
  everywhere kindness.
Jesus, our Lord,
  lead us and guide us,
best of all friends,
  always beside us.

H. C. A. GAUNT (b. 1902)

SECOND TUNE

Little Venice 4 5.4 5.D.   Gerald H. Knight (1908–79)

Best of all friends

1

Jesus, my Lord,
  let me be near you;
by your own word
  help me to hear you.
Jesus, my Lord,
  lead me to love you,
nothing more dear,
  no one above you.

2

All through the day,
  sisters and brothers,
yours we will be,
  caring for others,
hearing your words,
  learning your story,
bearing your cross,
  sharing your glory.

3

Teach us to know
  seeing from blindness,
help us to show
  everywhere kindness.
Jesus, our Lord,
  lead us and guide us,
best of all friends,
  always beside us.

H. C. A. Gaunt (b. 1902)

The Supper of the Lamb

Jesus, we thus obey
    thy last and kindest word;
here in thine own appointed way
    we come to meet thee, Lord.

2

Our hearts we open wide
    to make the Saviour room;
and lo, the Lamb, the Crucified,
    the sinner's friend, is come.

3

Thy presence makes the feast;
    now let our spirits feel
the glory not to be expressed,
    the joy unspeakable.

4

With high and heavenly bliss
    thou dost our spirits cheer;
thy house of banqueting is this
    and thou hast brought us here.

5

Now let our souls be fed
    with manna from above,
and over us thy banner spread
    of everlasting love.

CHARLES WESLEY* (1707–88)

The Holy Spirit and the Church

Let every Christian pray,
this day, and every day,
   Come, Holy Spirit, come.
Was not the Church we love
commissioned from above?
   Come, Holy Spirit, come.

2

The Spirit brought to birth
the Church of Christ on earth
   to seek and save the lost:
never has he withdrawn,
since that tremendous dawn,
   his gifts at Pentecost.

3

Age after age, he strove
to teach her how to love:
   come, Holy Spirit, come;
age after age, anew
she proved the gospel true:
   come, Holy Spirit, come.

4

Only the Spirit's power
can fit us for this hour:
   come, Holy Spirit, come;
instruct, inspire, unite;
and make us see the light:
   come, Holy Spirit, come.

F. PRATT GREEN (b. 1903)

146 Chartres (Angers) 11 11 11.5.

Melody from *Chartres Antiphoner, 1784*

Unison

The Lord's own

Let the Lord's People, heart and voice uniting,
praise him who calls them out of sin and darkness
into his own light, that he may create them
  his holy priesthood.

2

This is the Lord's House, home of all his people,
school for the faithful, refuge for the sinner,
rest for the pilgrim, haven for the weary;
  all find a welcome.

3

This is the Lord's Day, day of God's own making,
day of creation, day of resurrection,
day of the Spirit, Pentecost repeated,
  day for rejoicing.

4

In the Lord's Service bread and wine are offered,
that Christ may take them, bless them, break and give them
to all his people, his own life imparting,
  food everlasting.

JOHN E. BOWERS (b. 1923)

Unison

Refrain

Have mercy

Let us break bread together on our knees;
let us break bread together on our knees:

when I fall on my knees
with my face to the rising sun,
O Lord, have mercy, if you please.

2

Let us drink wine together on our knees;
let us drink wine together on our knees:

when I fall on my knees
with my face to the rising sun,
O Lord, have mercy, if you please.

3

Let us praise God together on our knees;
let us praise God together on our knees:

when I fall on my knees
with my face to the rising sun,
O Lord, have mercy, if you please.

American Folk Hymn

148 Linstead L.M. and Refrain

Jamaican Folk Song,
adapted by Doreen Potter

Unison

Refrain

Communion Calypso

Let us talents and tongues employ,
reaching out with a shout of joy:
bread is broken, the wine is poured,
Christ is spoken and seen and heard:

Jesus lives again, earth can breathe again,
pass the Word around: loaves abound.

2

Christ is able to make us one,
at his table he sets the tone,
teaching people to live to bless,
love in word and in deed express:

Jesus lives again, earth can breathe again,
pass the Word around: loaves abound.

3

Jesus calls us in, sends us out
bearing fruit in a world of doubt,
gives us love to tell, bread to share:
God-Immanuel everywhere:

Jesus lives again, earth can breathe again,
pass the Word around: loaves abound.

FRED KAAN (b. 1929)

149 Litherop 8 7.8 7.8 7.   Peter Cutts (b. 1937)

Unison

A song of love and living

Life is great! So sing about it,
  as we can and as we should –
shops and buses, towns and people,
  village, farmland, field and wood.
Life is great and life is given;
  life is lovely, free and good.

2

Life is great! – whatever happens,
  snow or sunshine, joy or pain,
hardship, grief or disillusion,
  suffering that I can't explain –
life is great if someone loves me,
  holds my hand and calls my name.

3

Love is great! – the love of lovers,
  whispered words and longing eyes;
love that gazes at the cradle
  where a child of loving lies;
love that lasts when youth has faded,
  bends with age, but never dies.

4

Love is giving and receiving –
  boy and girl, or friend with friend;
love is bearing and forgiving
  all the hurts that hate can send;
love's the greatest way of living,
  hoping, trusting to the end.

5

God is great! In Christ he loved us,
  as we should, but never can –
love that suffered, hoped and trusted
  when disciples turned and ran,
love that broke through death for ever.
  Praise that loving, living Man!

BRIAN A. WREN (b. 1936)

Truro L.M.

Melody from T. Williams's
Psalmodia Evangelica, 1789

The Coming of Christ

Lift up your heads, you mighty gates,
behold, the King of Glory waits,
  the King of kings is drawing near,
  the Saviour of the world is here.

2

O blest the land, the city blest
where Christ the ruler is confessed.
  O happy hearts and happy homes
  to whom this King in triumph comes.

3

Fling wide the portals of your heart,
make it a temple set apart
  from earthly use for heaven's employ,
  adorned with prayer and love and joy.

4

Come, Saviour, come, with us abide;
our hearts to thee we open wide:
  thy Holy Spirit guide us on,
  until our glorious goal is won.

GEORG WEISSEL (1590–1635)
tr. CATHERINE WINKWORTH* (1827–78)

151 Personent hodie   6 6.6 6 6. and Refrain

Melody from *Piae Cantiones*, 1582

Unison

Refrain

* *Last verse only.*

Jesus comes

Long ago, prophets knew
Christ would come, born a Jew,
come to make all things new,
bear his people's burden,
freely love and pardon.

Ring, bells, ring, ring, ring!
Sing, choirs, sing, sing, sing!
When he comes,
when he comes,
who will make him welcome?

2

God in time, God in man,
this is God's timeless plan:
he will come, as a man,
born himself of woman,
God divinely human:

3

Mary, hail! Though afraid,
she believed, she obeyed.
In her womb God is laid,
till the time expected,
nurtured and protected:

4

Journey ends: where afar
Bethlem shines, like a star,
stable door stands ajar.
Unborn Son of Mary,
Saviour, do not tarry.

Ring, bells, ring, ring, ring!
Sing, choirs, sing, sing, sing!
Jesus comes,
Jesus comes:
we will make him welcome.

F. PRATT GREEN (b. 1903)

152 Ainsdale L.M.

John M. Etherton (b. 1939)

Our wills are ours, to make them thine

Lord, as I wake I turn to you,
　　yourself the first thought of my day:
my King, my God, whose help is sure,
　　yourself the help for which I pray.

2

There is no blessing, Lord, from you
　　for those who make their will their way;
no praise for those who will not praise,
　　no peace for those who will not pray.

3

Your loving gifts of grace to me,
　　those favours I could never earn,
call for my thanks in praise and prayer,
　　call me to love you in return.

4

Lord, make my life a life of love,
　　keep me from sin in all I do;
Lord, make your law my only law,
　　your will my will, for love of you.

BRIAN FOLEY (b. 1919)
Psalm 5

153 Stonegate 11 10.11 10.

Cyril V. Taylor (b. 1907)

Harvest

Lord, by whose breath all souls and seeds are living
   with life that is and life that is to be,
fruits of the earth we offer with thanksgiving
   for fields in flood with summer's golden sea.

2

Lord of the earth, accept these gifts in token
   thou in thy works art to be all-adored,
from whom the light as daily bread is broken,
   sunset and dawn as wine and milk are poured.

3

Poor is our praise, but these shall be our psalter;
   lo, like thyself they rose up from the dead;
Lord, give them back when at thy holy altar
   we feed on thee, who art our living bread.

ANDREW YOUNG* (1885–1971)

154   Abingdon   8 8.8 8.8 8.   Erik Routley (b. 1917)

Through Christ . . a living sacrifice

Lord Christ, we praise your sacrifice,
   your life in love so freely given:
for those who took your life away
   you prayed, that they might be forgiven;
and there, in helplessness arrayed,
God's power was perfectly displayed.

2

Once helpless in your mother's arms,
   dependent on her mercy then,
you made yourself again, by choice,
   as helpless in the hands of men;
and, at their mercy crucified,
you claimed your victory and died.

3

Though helpless and rejected then,
   you're now as reigning Lord acclaimed;
for ever by your victory
   is God's eternal love proclaimed –
the love which goes through death to find
new life and hope for all mankind.

4

So, living Lord, prepare us now
   your willing helplessness to share;
to give ourselves in sacrifice
   to overcome the world's despair;
in love to give our lives away
and claim your victory today.

ALAN GAUNT (b. 1935)

Unison

God's Saints

Lord God, we give you thanks for all your saints
    who sought the trackless footprints of your feet,
who took into their own a hand unseen
    and heard a voice whose silence was complete.

2

In every word and deed they spoke of Christ,
    and in their life gave glory to his name;
their love was unconsumed, a burning bush
    of which the Holy Spirit was the flame.

3

Blest Trinity, may yours be endless praise
    for all who lived so humbly in your sight;
your holy ones who walked dark ways in faith
    now share the joy of your unfailing light.

MARCELLA MARTIN (b. 1908)

156 Ryburn 8 8.8 8.8 8. Norman Cocker (1889–1953)

By grace alone

Lord God, your love has called us here,
    as we, by love, for love were made.
Your living likeness still we bear,
    though marred, dishonoured, disobeyed.
We come, with all our heart and mind
your call to hear, your love to find.

*2

We come with self-inflicted pains
    of broken trust and chosen wrong,
half-free, half-bound by inner chains,
    by social forces swept along,
by powers and systems close confined,
yet seeking hope for humankind.

3

Lord God, in Christ you call our name,
    and then receive us as your own,
not through some merit, right or claim,
    but by your gracious love alone.
We strain to glimpse your mercy-seat,
and find you kneeling at our feet.

4

Then take the towel, and break the bread,
    and humble us, and call us friends.
Suffer and serve till all are fed,
    and show how grandly love intends
to work till all creation sings,
to fill all worlds, to crown all things.

*5

Lord God, in Christ you set us free
    your life to live, your joy to share.
Give us your Spirit's liberty
    to turn from guilt and dull despair
and offer all that faith can do,
while love is making all things new.

BRIAN A. WREN (b. 1936)

R. R. Terry (1865–1938)

The excellency and variety of Scripture

Lord, I have made thy word my choice,
   my lasting heritage:
there shall my noblest powers rejoice,
   my warmest thoughts engage.

2

I'll read the histories of thy love,
   and keep thy laws in sight,
while through thy promises I rove
   with ever-fresh delight.

3

'Tis a broad land of wealth unknown,
   where springs of life arise,
seeds of immortal bliss are sown,
   and hidden glory lies.

Isaac Watts* (1674–1748)
from Psalm 119

158 Niagara L.M.   Robert Jackson (1840–1914)

Before reading the Scriptures

Lord Jesus Christ, be present now,
and let your Holy Spirit bow⏝
all hearts in love and fear today
to hear the truth and keep your way.

2

Open our lips to sing your praise,
our hearts in true devotion raise,
strengthen our faith, increase our light,
that we may know your name aright.

Anon, German
tr. CATHERINE WINKWORTH* (1827–78)

159

Guarda   7 7 7.5.   Sydney Watson (b. 1903)

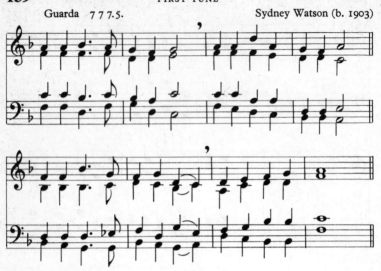

Huddersfield   7 7 7.5.   Walter Parratt (1841–1924)

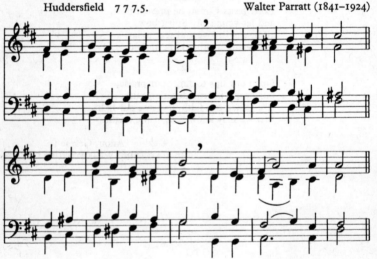

Hear and save

Lord of all, to whom alone
all our hearts' desires are known,
when we stand before thy throne,
    Jesu, hear and save.

2

Son of Man, before whose eyes
every secret open lies,
at thy great and last assize,
    Jesu, hear and save.

3

Son of God, whose angel host
(thou hast said) rejoiceth most
o'er the sinner who was lost,
    Jesu, hear and save.

4

Saviour, who didst not condemn
those who touched thy garments' hem,
mercy show to us and them:
    Jesu, hear and save.

5

Lord, the Way to sinners shown,
Lord, the Truth by sinners known,
Love Incarnate on the throne,
    Jesu, hear and save.

C. A. ALINGTON (1872–1955)

San Rocco   C.M.   Derek Williams (b. 1945)

Unison

Creator and Redeemer

1

Lord of the boundless curves of space
   and time's deep mystery,
to your creative might we trace
   all nature's energy.

2

Your mind conceived the galaxy,
   each atom's secret planned,
and every age of history
   your purpose, Lord, has spanned.

3

Your Spirit gave the living cell
   its hidden, vital force:
the instincts which all life impel
   derive from you, their source.

4

Yours is the image stamped on man,
   though marred by man's own sin;
and yours the liberating plan
   again his soul to win.

5

Science explores your reason's ways,
   and faith can this impart
that in the face of Christ our gaze
   looks deep within your heart.

6

Christ is your wisdom's perfect word,
   your mercy's crowning deed:
in him the sons of earth have heard
   your strong compassion plead.

7

Give us to know your truth; but more,
   the strength to do your will;
until the love our souls adore
   shall all our being fill.

ALBERT F. BAYLY (b. 1901)

London New   C.M.

Scottish Psalter, 1635
as adapted in Playford's *Psalms*, 1671

Creator and Redeemer

1

Lord of the boundless curves of space
    and time's deep mystery,
to your creative might we trace⌣
    all nature's energy.

2

Your mind conceived the galaxy,
    each atom's secret planned,
and every age of history
    your purpose, Lord, has spanned.

3

Your Spirit gave the living cell⌣
    its hidden, vital force:
the instincts which all life impel
    derive from you, their source.

4

Yours is the image stamped on man,
    though marred by man's own sin;
and yours the liberating plan
    again his soul to win.

5

Science explores your reason's ways,
    and faith can this impart
that in the face of Christ our gaze⌣
    looks deep within your heart.

6

Christ is your wisdom's perfect word,
    your mercy's crowning deed:
in him the sons of earth have heard⌣
    your strong compassion plead.

7

Give us to know your truth; but more,
    the strength to do your will;
until the love our souls adore
    shall all our being fill.

ALBERT F. BAYLY (b. 1901)

161 Warrington L.M.   R. Harrison (1748–1810)

Our homes

Lord of the home, your only Son
   received a mother's tender love,
and from an earthly father won
   his vision of your home above.

2

Help us, O Lord, our homes to make
   your Holy Spirit's dwelling place;
our hands' and hearts' devotion take
   to be the servants of your grace.

3

Teach us to keep our homes so fair
   that, were our Lord a child once more,
he might be glad our hearth to share,
   and find a welcome at our door.

4

Lord, may your Spirit sanctify
   each household duty we fulfil;
may we our Master glorify
   in glad obedience to your will.

ALBERT F. BAYLY (b. 1901)

Rex gloriae 8 7.8 7.D.   H. Smart (1813–79)

Offerings

Lord, to you we bring our treasure,
    wealth of mind and hand and heart,
fruit of toil and joy of leisure,
    music, word, and craftsman's art,
truths of prophets, saints, and sages,
    patient skills of hearth and home;
Father, giver down the ages,
    these are yours; to you we come.

2

Jesus, Servant, in your passion
    offering all for all mankind,
teach us in ourselves to fashion
    day by day your will, your mind,
live for truth, for justice striving,
    heal the sick, the hungry feed,
by your work, your words, your giving
    set to help all human need.

3

In your sacrament now sharing
    round your table, risen Lord,
each for every other caring,
    wrongs forgiven, faith restored,
bread and wine of life receiving,
    yours the Body, yours the Blood,
may we be your Church believing,
    one in worldwide brotherhood.

H. C. A. GAUNT (b. 1902)

163 Song 13   7 7.7 7.

Melody and bass by
Orlando Gibbons (1583–1625)

Alternative Tune: *Vienna* (HT 47; A.M.R. 44; E.H. 500; S.P. 357)

Love's endeavour, love's expense

Morning glory, starlit sky,
  soaring music, scholars' truth,
flight of swallows, autumn leaves,
  memory's treasure, grace of youth:

2

open are the gifts of God,
  gifts of love to mind and sense;
hidden is love's agony,
  love's endeavour, love's expense.

3

Love that gives, gives ever more,
  gives with zeal, with eager hands,
spares not, keeps not, all outpours,
  ventures all, its all expends.

4

Drained is love in making full,
  bound in setting others free,
poor in making many rich,
  weak in giving power to be.

5

Therefore he who shows us God
  helpless hangs upon the tree;
and the nails and crown of thorns
  tell of what God's love must be.

6

Here is God: no monarch he,
  throned in easy state to reign;
here is God, whose arms of love
  aching, spent, the world sustain.

W. H. VANSTONE (b. 1923)

164 Nürnberg   L.M.

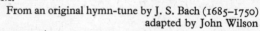

Christ crucified, the wisdom and power of God

Nature with open volume stands
    to spread her maker's praise abroad,
and every labour of his hands
    shows something worthy of our God.

2

But in the grace that rescued man
    his brightest form of glory shines;
here on the Cross 'tis fairest drawn
    in precious blood and crimson lines.

3

Here his whole name appears complete;
    nor wit can guess, nor reason prove
which of the letters best is writ,
    the power, the wisdom, or the love.

4

O the sweet wonders of that Cross
    where God the Saviour loved and died;
her noblest life my spirit draws
    from his dear wounds and bleeding side.

5

I would for ever speak his name
    in sounds to mortal ears unknown,
with angels join to praise the Lamb,
    and worship at his Father's throne.

ISAAC WATTS* (1674–1748)

165 Rendez à Dieu 9 8.9 8.D.

Melody from *La Forme des Prières*,
Strasbourg, 1545
(2nd line as in *Genevan Psalter* of 1551)

1 New songs of ce - le - bra - tion ren - der to him who
2 Joy - ful - ly, heart - i - ly re - sound - ing, let ev' - ry
3 Ri - vers and seas and tor - rents roar - ing, hon - our the

has great won - ders done. Love sits en - throned in age - less splend - our:
in - stru - ment and voice peal out the praise of grace a - bound - ing,
Lord with wild ac - claim; moun - tains and stones look up a - dor - ing

come and a - dore the migh - ty one. He has made known his great sal -
call - ing the whole world to re - joice. Trum - pets and or - gans, set in
and find a voice to praise his name. Right - eous, com - mand - ing, ev - er

A joyful noise

1

New songs of celebration render
    to him who has great wonders done.
Love sits enthroned in ageless splendour:
    come and adore the mighty one.
He has made known his great salvation
    which all his friends with joy confess:
he has revealed to every nation
    his everlasting righteousness.

2

Joyfully, heartily resounding,
    let every instrument and voice
peal out the praise of grace abounding,
    calling the whole world to rejoice.
Trumpets and organs, set in motion
    such sounds as make the heavens ring;
all things that live in earth and ocean,
    make music for your mighty King.

3

Rivers and seas and torrents roaring,
    honour the Lord with wild acclaim;
mountains and stones look up adoring
    and find a voice to praise his name.
Righteous, commanding, ever glorious,
    praises be his that never cease:
just is our God, whose truth victorious
    establishes the world in peace.

ERIK ROUTLEY (b. 1917)
Psalm 98

166 Glasgow C.M.   Moore's *Psalm-Singer's Pocket Companion,* 1756

Alternative Tune: *University* (A.M.R. 254; E.H. 93; S.P. 653)

A new day

Now from the altar of our hearts
  let incense flames arise;
assist us, Lord, to offer up
  our morning sacrifice.

2

Awake, my love; awake, my joy;
  awake, my heart and tongue.
Sleep not: when mercies loudly call,
  break forth into a song.

3

This day be God our sun and shield,
  our keeper and our guide;
his care be on our frailty shown,
  his mercies multiplied.

4

New time, new favour, and new joys
  a new song all require;
till we shall praise thee as we would,
  accept our hearts' desire.

JOHN MASON* (c. 1645–1694)

Geoffrey Laycock (b. 1927)

Unison

Harvest

Now join we, to praise the Creator,
    our voices in worship and song;
we stand to recall with thanksgiving
    that to him all seasons belong.

2

We thank you, O God, for your goodness,
    for the joy and abundance of crops,
for food that is stored in our larders,
    for all we can buy in the shops.

3

But also of need and starvation
    we sing with concern and despair,
of skills that are used for destruction,
    of land that is burnt and laid bare.

4

We cry for the plight of the hungry
    while harvests are left on the field,
for orchards neglected and wasting,
    for produce from markets withheld.

5

The song grows in depth and in wideness:
    the earth and its people are one.
There can be no thanks without giving,
    no words without deeds that are done.

6

Then teach us, O Lord of the harvest,
    to be humble in all that we claim:
to share what we have with the nations,
    to care for the world in your name.

FRED KAAN (b. 1929)

Noel nouvelet 11 10.10 11.

Old French Melody
Harmonies by Martin Shaw (1875–1958)

For another tune see over page

Life through death

Now the green blade riseth from the buried grain,
wheat that in dark earth many days has lain;
Love lives again, that with the dead has been:

  Love is come again,
  like wheat that springeth green.

2

In the grave they laid him, Love whom men had slain,
thinking that never he would wake again,
laid in the earth like grain that sleeps unseen:

3

Forth he came at Easter, like the risen grain,
he that for three days in the grave had lain,
quick from the dead my risen Lord is seen:

4

When our hearts are wintry, grieving, or in pain,
thy touch can call us back to life again,
fields of our hearts that dead and bare have been:

  Love is come again,
  like wheat that springeth green.

J. M. C. CRUM (1872–1958)

Green Blade 11 10.10 11. Greville Cooke (b. 1894)

Love is come a-gain, Love is come a-gain, like wheat that spring-eth green.

Life through death

Now the green blade riseth from the buried grain,
wheat that in dark earth many days has lain;
Love lives again, that with the dead has been:

    Love is come again,
    like wheat that springeth green.

2

In the grave they laid him, Love whom men had slain,
thinking that never he would wake again,
laid in the earth like grain that sleeps unseen:

3

Forth he came at Easter, like the risen grain,
he that for three days in the grave had lain,
quick from the dead my risen Lord is seen:

4

When our hearts are wintry, grieving, or in pain,
thy touch can call us back to life again,
fields of our hearts that dead and bare have been:

    Love is come again,
    like wheat that springeth green.

J. M. C. CRUM (1872–1958)

169 Crediton C.M.

Melody by Thomas Clark (1775–1859)
Harmonies by Martin Shaw (1875–1950)

Transfiguration

O raise your eyes on high and see,
    there stands our sovereign Lord;
his glory is this day revealed,
    his Word a two-edged sword.

2

We glimpse the splendour and the power
    of him who conquered death,
the Christ in whom the universe
    knows God's creating breath.

3

Of every creed and nation King
    in him all strife is stilled;
the promise made to Abraham
    in him has been fulfilled.

4

The prophets stand and with great joy
    give witness as they gaze;
the Father with a sign has sealed
    our trust, our hope, our praise.

RALPH WRIGHT (b. 1938)

Unison

Fruit of the Spirit

1

Of all the Spirit's gifts to me,
I pray that I may never cease
to take and treasure most these three:
    love, joy, and peace.

2

He shows me love is at the root
of every gift sent from above,
of every flower, of every fruit,
    that God is love.

3

He shows me that if I possess
a love no evil can destroy,
however great is my distress,
    that this is joy.

4

Though what's ahead is mystery,
and life itself is ours on lease,
each day the Spirit says to me,
    'Go forth in peace'.

5

We go in peace, but made aware
that in a needy world like this
our clearest purpose is to share
    love, joy, and peace.

F. PRATT GREEN (b. 1903)

Unison

Pentecost

<table>
<tr><td>

1

On the day of Pentecost,
  when the twelve assembled,
came on them the Holy Ghost
  in fire that tongues resembled.

2

In the power of God he came,
  as the Lord had told them,
in his blessèd, holy name
  with wisdom to uphold them.

</td><td>

3

In the Spirit then they stood
  to proclaim Christ dying,
and that he for all men's good
  doth live, true strength supplying.

4

Still the might by which we live
  from our God descendeth;
still his Spirit Christ doth give,
  who guideth and defendeth.

</td></tr>
</table>

5

Praise, O praise our heavenly King
  for his grace toward us;
gladly now his glory sing,
  who doth his power afford us.

T. C. HUNTER CLARE (b. 1910)

The family

1

Our Father, by whose name
  all fatherhood is known,
who in your love proclaim
  each family your own,
direct all parents, guarding well,
with constant love as sentinel,
the homes in which your people dwell.

2

Lord Christ, yourself a child
  within an earthly home,
with heart still undefiled
  you did to manhood come;
our children bless in every place,
that they may all behold your face,
and knowing you may grow in grace.

3

Blest Spirit, who can bind
  our hearts in unity,
and teach us so to find
  the love from self set free,
in all our hearts such love increase
that every home, by this release,
may be the dwelling place of peace.

F. BLAND TUCKER (b. 1895)

173 Coelites plaudant 11 11 11.5. Melody from *Rouen Antiphoner*, 1728
(Rouen) Harmonies by R. Vaughan Williams (1872–1958)

Unison

Baptism

Praise and thanksgiving be to our Creator,
source of this blessing: Father, Mediator,
baptize and make your own those who come before you,
    while we adore you.

2

Not our own holiness, nor that we have striven,
brings us the peace which you, O Christ, have given.
Baptize and set apart: come, O risen Saviour,
    with grace and favour.

3

Come, Holy Spirit, come in visitation:
you are the truth, our hope and our salvation.
Baptize with joy and power: give, O Dove descending,
    life never ending.

HAROLD FRANCIS YARDLEY (b. 1911)
FRANK J. WHITELEY (b. 1914)

Offertory

Reap me the earth as a harvest to God,
  gather and bring it again,
all that is his, to the maker of all;
  lift it and offer it high.

  Bring bread, bring wine,
    give glory to the Lord;
  whose is the earth but God's,
    whose is the praise but his?

2

Go with your song and your music, with joy,
  go to the altar of God;
carry your offerings, fruits of the earth,
  work of your labouring hands:

3

Gladness and pity and passion and pain,
  all that is mortal in man,
lay all before him, return him his gift,
  God, to whom all shall go home.

  Bring bread, bring wine,
    give glory to the Lord;
  whose is the earth but God's,
    whose is the praise but his?

'PETER ICARUS'

God's Saints

Rejoice in God's saints, today and all days:
a world without saints forgets how to praise.
   Their faith in acquiring the habit of prayer,
   their depth of adoring, Lord, help us to share.

2

Some march with events to turn them God's way;
some need to withdraw, the better to pray;
   some carry the gospel through fire and through flood:
   our world is their parish; their purpose is God.

3

Rejoice in those saints, unpraised and unknown,
who bear someone's cross or shoulder their own;
   they shame our complaining, our comforts, our cares:
   what patience in caring, what courage, is theirs!

4

Rejoice in God's saints, today and all days:
a world without saints forgets how to praise.
   In loving, in living, they prove it is true –
   the way of self-giving, Lord, leads us to you.

F. PRATT GREEN (b. 1903)

Sussex 8 7.8 7.

English Traditional Melody
adapted by R. Vaughan Williams (1872–1958)

The word of the Lord

Rise and hear! The Lord is speaking,
    as the gospel words unfold;
man, in all his agelong seeking,
    finds no firmer truth to hold.

2

Word of goodness, truth, and beauty,
    heard by simple folk and wise,
word of freedom, word of duty,
    word of life beyond our eyes.

3

Word of God's forgiveness granted
    to the wild or guilty soul,
word of love that works undaunted,
    changes, heals, and makes us whole.

4

Speak to us, O Lord, believing,
    as we hear, the sower sows;
may our hearts, your word receiving,
    be the good ground where it grows.

H. C. A. GAUNT (b. 1902)

Great Wilkins   8 7.8 7.   Ian A. Copley (b. 1926)

Unison

The word of the Lord

1

Rise and hear! The Lord is speaking,
  as the gospel words unfold;
man, in all his agelong seeking,
  finds no firmer truth to hold.

2

Word of goodness, truth, and beauty,
  heard by simple folk and wise,
word of freedom, word of duty,
  word of life beyond our eyes.

3

Word of God's forgiveness granted
  to the wild or guilty soul,
word of love that works undaunted,
  changes, heals, and makes us whole.

4

Speak to us, O Lord, believing,
  as we hear, the sower sows;
may our hearts, your word receiving,
  be the good ground where it grows.

H. C. A. GAUNT (b. 1902)

After Communion

Sent forth by God's blessing, our true faith confessing,
   the People of God from his dwelling take leave.
The supper is ended: O now be extended
   the fruits of his service in all who believe.
The seed of his teaching, our hungry souls reaching,
   shall blossom in action for God and for man.
His grace shall incite us, his love shall unite us
   to work for his kingdom and further his plan.

2

With praise and thanksgiving to God everliving,
   the task of our everyday life we will face,
our faith ever sharing, in love ever caring,
   embracing as brothers all men of each race.
One feast that has fed us, one light that has led us,
   unite us as one in his life that we share.
Then may all the living, with praise and thanksgiving,
   give honour to Christ and his name that we bear.

OMER WESTENDORF (b. 1916)

John Dykes Bower (b. 1905)

Alternative Tune: *Westminster* (A.M.R. 169; E.H. 441; S.P. 581)

The Saviour

The great Creator of the worlds,
   the sovereign God of heaven,
his holy and immortal truth
   to men on earth has given.

2

He sent no angel of his host
   to bear his mighty word,
but him through whom the worlds were made,
   the everlasting Lord.

3

He sent him not in wrath and power,
   but grace and peace to bring;
in kindness, as a king might send
   his son, himself a king.

4

He sent him down as sending God;
   as man he came to men;
as one with us he dwelt with us,
   and died and lives again.

5

He came as Saviour to his own,
   the way of love he trod;
he came to win men by good will,
   for force is not of God.

6

Not to oppress, but summon men
   their truest life to find,
in love God sent his Son to save,
   not to condemn mankind.

From *Epistle to Diognetus* (2nd cent.)
tr. F. BLAND TUCKER (b. 1895)

179 Wolvercote 7 6.7 6.D.   W. H. Ferguson (1874–1950)

Unison

The Kingdom of God

'The kingdom is upon you!'
    the voice of Jesus cries,
fulfilling with its message
    the wisdom of the wise;
it lightens with fresh insight
    the striving human mind,
creating new dimensions
    of purpose for mankind.

2

'God's kingdom is upon you!'
    The message sounds today,
it summons every pilgrim
    to take the questing way,
with eyes intent on Jesus,
    our leader and our friend,
who trod faith's road before us,
    and trod it to the end.

3

The kingdom is upon us!
    Stirred by the Spirit's breath,
we glory in its freedom
    from emptiness and death;
we celebrate its purpose,
    its mission and its goal,
alive with the conviction
    that Christ can make us whole.

ROBERT WILLIS (b. 1947)

180 Forgive our sins   C.M.   American Folk Hymn Melody in
A Supplement to the Kentucky Harmony, 1820

Alternative Tune: *St. Stephen* (A.M.R. 424; E.H. 337; S.P. 250)

The Gospel

The prophets spoke in days of old
  to men of stubborn will.
Their message lives and is retold
  where hearts are stubborn still.

2

And Jesus spoke to sinful men
  of love, of joy, of peace.
His message lives, he speaks again,
  and sinners find release.

3

Shall we not hear that message, Lord,
  to lead us on the way?
Come, Christ, make plain your saving word,
  and speak to us today.

JOHN E. BOWERS (b. 1923)

181 Diva servatrix 11 11 11.5.   Melody from *Bayeux Antiphoner*, 1739

Unison

The tree of life

There in God's garden stands the tree of wisdom
whose leaves hold forth the healing of the nations:
tree of all knowledge, tree of all compassion,
    tree of all beauty.

2

Its name is Jesus, name that says 'Our Saviour':
there on its branches see the scars of suffering:
see where the tendrils of our human selfhood
    feed on its lifeblood.

3

Thorns not its own are tangled in its foliage;
our greed has starved it, our despite has choked it;
yet, look, it lives! its grief has not destroyed it,
    nor fire consumed it.

4

See how its branches reach to us in welcome;
hear what the voice says, 'Come to me, ye weary:
'give me your sickness, give me all your sorrow:
    I will give blessing.'

5

All heaven is singing, 'Thanks to Christ whose passion
offers in mercy healing, strength and pardon:
peoples and nations, take it, take it freely'.
    Amen, my Master.

ERIK ROUTLEY (1974)
based on a hymn by
PECSELYI KIRALY IMRE (1961)

182 Lauds 7 7. 7 7.   John Wilson (b. 1905)

Optional descant for verses 4 and 7

Praise___ the love!_____   Praise___ the

love!_____   Al_____le__lu_____ia!

Al_____le__lu_____ia!_____

(small notes organ only)

Praise the Holy Spirit

There's a spirit in the air,
telling Christians everywhere:
   'Praise the love that Christ revealed,
   living, working, in our world'.

2

Lose your shyness, find your tongue,
tell the world what God has done:
   God in Christ has come to stay;
   we can see his power today.

3

When believers break the bread,
when a hungry child is fed,
   praise the love that Christ revealed,
   living, working, in our world.

4

Still his Spirit leads the fight,
seeing wrong and setting right:
   God in Christ has come to stay;
   we can see his power today.

5

When a stranger's not alone,
where the homeless find a home,
   praise the love that Christ revealed,
   living, working, in our world.

6

May his Spirit fill our praise,
guide our thoughts and change our ways.
   God in Christ has come to stay;
   we can see his power today.

7

There's a Spirit in the air,
calling people everywhere:
   Praise the love that Christ revealed,
   living, working, in our world.

BRIAN A. WREN (b. 1936)

Cyril V. Taylor (b. 1907)

Unison

In verse 2 or 3 the choir may hum or vocalize the harmony

St Patrick's Breastplate

This day God gives me
strength of high heaven,
sun and moon shining,
  flame in my hearth;
flashing of lightning,
wind in its swiftness,
deeps of the ocean,
  firmness of earth.

2

This day God sends me
strength as my steersman,
might to uphold me,
  wisdom as guide.
Your eyes are watchful,
your ears are listening,
your lips are speaking,
  friend at my side.

3

God's way is my way,
God's shield is round me,
God's host defends me,
  saving from ill;
angels of heaven,
drive from me always
all that would harm me,
  stand by me still.

4

Rising, I thank you,
mighty and strong one,
king of creation,
  giver of rest,
firmly confessing
threeness of Persons,
oneness of Godhead,
  Trinity blest.

JAMES QUINN (b. 1919)
from 8th century Irish

FIRST TUNE

St. Mary C.M.   Melody from E. Prys's *Llyfr y Psalmau*, 1621
                              Harmony based on setting in Playford's *Psalms*, 1677

Wigtown C.M.   Melody, and most of the harmony,
                              from *Scottish Psalter*, 1635

It is intended that the first half of each verse shall be sung to *St. Mary*
and the second half to *Wigtown*

For another tune see over page

Royal Insignia

To mock your reign, O dearest Lord,
　　they made a crown of thorns;
set you with taunts along that road
　　from which no man returns.
They could not know, as we do now,
　　how glorious is that crown:
that thorns would flower upon your brow,
　　your sorrows heal our own.

2

In mock acclaim, O gracious Lord,
　　they snatched a purple cloak,
your passion turned, for all they cared,
　　into a soldier's joke.
They could not know, as we do now,
　　that, though we merit blame,
you will your robe of mercy throw
　　around our naked shame.

3

A sceptred reed, O patient Lord,
　　they thrust into your hand,
and acted out their grim charade
　　to its appointed end.
They could not know, as we do now,
　　though empires rise and fall,
your kingdom shall not cease to grow
　　till love embraces all.

F. Pratt Green (b. 1903)

184 *(continued)*

Third Mode Melody D.C.M.

Thomas Tallis (c. 1515–85)
edited by John Wilson

Unison or Harmony

1 To mock your reign, O dear-est Lord, they made a crown of thorns;
2 In mock ac-claim, O gra-cious Lord, they snatched a pur-ple cloak,
3 A scep-tred reed, O pa-tient Lord, they thrust in-to your hand,

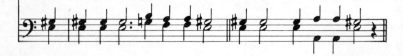

set   you with taunts a-long that road from which no man re-turns.
your   pas-sion turned, for all they cared, in-to a sol-dier's joke.
and   act-ed out their grim cha-rade to its ap-poin-ted end.

They could not— know, as we do now, how glo-rious is that crown:
They could not— know, as we do now, that, though we me-rit blame,
They could not— know, as we do now, though em-pires rise and fall,

that thorns would flower up-on your brow, your sor-rows heal our own.
you will your robe of mer - cy throw a-round our na-ked shame.
your king - dom shall not cease to grow till love em-bra-ces all.

Royal Insignia

To mock your reign, O dearest Lord,
   they made a crown of thorns;
set you with taunts along that road
   from which no man returns.
They could not know, as we do now,
   how glorious is that crown:
that thorns would flower upon your brow,
   your sorrows heal our own.

2

In mock acclaim, O gracious Lord,
   they snatched a purple cloak,
your passion turned, for all they cared,
   into a soldier's joke.
They could not know, as we do now,
   that, though we merit blame,
you will your robe of mercy throw
   around our naked shame.

3

A sceptred reed, O patient Lord,
   they thrust into your hand,
and acted out their grim charade
   to its appointed end.
They could not know, as we do now,
   though empires rise and fall,
your kingdom shall not cease to grow
   till love embraces all.

F. PRATT GREEN (b. 1903)

The words were written for this tune

Au clair de la lune   6 5 6 5.6 5 7 5.   French Traditional Melody

Unison

Gardens

Walking in a garden
  at the close of day,
Adam tried to hide him
  when he heard God say:
'Why are you so frightened,
  why are you afraid?
You have brought the winter in,
  made the flowers fade.'

2

Walking in a garden
  where the Lord had gone,
three of the disciples,
  Peter, James, and John;
they were very weary,
  could not keep awake,
while the Lord was kneeling there,
  praying for their sake.

3

Walking in a garden
  at the break of day,
Mary asked the gardener
  where the body lay;
but he turned towards her,
  smiled at her and said:
'Mary, spring is here to stay,
  only death is dead.'

HILARY GREENWOOD (b. 1929)

186 Whitfield 5 4.5 5.7.   John Wilson (b. 1905)

Optional descant for last verse

6 Lord, _____ in diff' - rent ways,

Unison

may all we're do - ing show that you're liv - ing, meet-

-ing your love with our praise. _____

first and last verses | verses 2 to 5

Ministers of Christ

We are your people:
Lord, by your grace,
   you dare to make us
   Christ to our neighbours
of every nation and race.

2

How can we demonstrate
your love and care?
   speaking or listening?
   battling or serving?
help us to know when and where.

3

Called to portray you,
help us to live
   closer than neighbours,
   open to strangers,
able to clash and forgive.

4

Glad of tradition,
help us to see
   in all life's changing
   where you are leading,
where our best efforts should be.

5

Joined in community,
breaking your bread,
   may we discover
   gifts in each other,
willing to lead and be led.

6

Lord, as we minister
in different ways,
   may all we're doing
   show that you're living,
meeting your love with our praise.

BRIAN A. WREN (b. 1936)

Melody and bass by
William Croft (1678–1727)

A Song of Praise
to the Blessed Trinity

We give immortal praise
to God the Father's love
for all our comforts here
and better hopes above:
    he sent his own
    eternal Son,
    to die for sins
    that man had done.

2

To God the Son belongs
immortal glory too,
who bought us with his blood
from everlasting woe:
    and now he lives,
    and now he reigns,
    and sees the fruit
    of all his pains.

3

To God the Spirit's name
immortal worship give,
whose new-creating power
makes the dead sinner live:
    his work completes
    the great design,
    and fills the soul
    with joy divine.

4

Almighty God, to thee
be endless honours done,
the undivided Three,
and the mysterious One:
    where reason fails
    with all her powers,
    there faith prevails,
    and love adores.

ISAAC WATTS* (1674–1748)

188 Crucis victoria   C.M.

M. B. Foster (1851–1922)

Baptized into Christ

We praise you, Lord, for Jesus Christ
  who died and rose again;
he lives to break the power of sin,
  and over death to reign.

2

We praise you that this child now shares
  the freedom Christ can give,
has died to sin with Christ, and now
  with Christ is raised to live.

3

We praise you, Lord, that now this child
  is grafted to the vine,
is made a member of your house
  and bears the cross as sign.

4

We praise you, Lord, for Jesus Christ;
  he loves this child we bring:
he frees, forgives, and heals us all,
  he lives and reigns as King.

JUDITH BEATRICE O'NEILL (b. 1930)

FIRST TUNE

Intercessor 11 10.11 10.   C. Hubert H. Parry (1848–1918)

For another tune see over page

The family of nations

We turn to you, O God of every nation,
  giver of life and origin of good;
your love is at the heart of all creation,
  your hurt is people's broken brotherhood.

2

We turn to you, that we may be forgiven
  for crucifying Christ on earth again.
We know that we have never wholly striven,
  forgetting self, to love the other man.

3

Free every heart from pride and self-reliance,
  our ways of thought inspire with simple grace;
break down among us barriers of defiance,
  speak to the soul of all the human race.

4

On men who fight on earth for right relations
  we pray the light of love from hour to hour.
Grant wisdom to the leaders of the nations,
  the gift of carefulness to those in power.

5

Teach us, good Lord, to serve the need of others,
  help us to give and not to count the cost.
Unite us all; for we are born as brothers:
  defeat our Babel with your Pentecost.

FRED KAAN (b. 1929)

Harding 11 10.11 10.   Cyril V. Taylor (b. 1907)

The family of nations

We turn to you, O God of every nation,
    giver of life and origin of good;
your love is at the heart of all creation,
    your hurt is people's broken brotherhood.

2

We turn to you, that we may be forgiven
    for crucifying Christ on earth again.
We know that we have never wholly striven,
    forgetting self, to love the other man.

3

Free every heart from pride and self-reliance,
    our ways of thought inspire with simple grace;
break down among us barriers of defiance,
    speak to the soul of all the human race.

4

On men who fight on earth for right relations
    we pray the light of love from hour to hour.
Grant wisdom to the leaders of the nations,
    the gift of carefulness to those in power.

5

Teach us, good Lord, to serve the need of others,
    help us to give and not to count the cost.
Unite us all, for we are born as brothers:
    defeat our Babel with your Pentecost.

FRED KAAN (b. 1929)

American Folk Hymn Melody
arr. Francis B. Westbrook (1903–75)

Melody

1 Were you there when they cru-ci-fied my Lord? _____
2 Were you there when they nailed him to the tree? _____
3 Were you there when they laid him in the tomb? _____

Harmony (Sopranos sing words above).

1 Were you there when they cru-ci-fied my Lord, were you
2 Were you there when they nailed him to the tree, were you
3 Were you there when they laid him in the tomb, were you

_____ Were you there when they cru-ci-fied my
_____ Were you there when they nailed him to the
_____ Were you there when they laid him in the

there? Were you there when they cru-ci-fied my
there? Were you there when they nailed him to the
there? Were you there when they laid him in the

Lord? _____
tree? _____ } Oh, _____
tomb? _____

Lord? when they cru-ci-fied my Lord? } Oh, _____
tree? when they nailed him to the tree?
tomb? when they laid him in the tomb?

Sometimes it caus-es me to tremble, tremble, tremble; }

Sometimes it caus-es me to tremble, tremble, tremble; }

continued over page

Were you there when they cru - ci - fied my Lord?
Were you there when they nailed him to the tree?
Were you there when they laid him in the tomb?

Were you there when they cru - ci - fied my Lord?
Were you there when they nailed him to the tree?
Were you there when they laid him in the tomb?

Were you there?

Were you there when they crucified my Lord?
Were you there when they crucified my Lord?
Oh, sometimes it causes me to tremble, tremble, tremble;
were you there when they crucified my Lord?

2

Were you there when they nailed him to the tree?
Were you there when they nailed him to the tree?
Oh, sometimes it causes me to tremble, tremble, tremble;
were you there when they nailed him to the tree?

3

Were you there when they laid him in the tomb?
Were you there when they laid him in the tomb?
Oh, sometimes it causes me to tremble, tremble, tremble;
were you there when they laid him in the tomb?

American Folk Hymn

191 Hermon 8 6.8 6 6.

Melody, and most of the bass,
by Jeremiah Clarke (1673–1707)

Adam and Christ

1

What Adam's disobedience cost,
  let holy scripture say:
mankind estranged, an Eden lost,
  and then a judgement day:
  each day a judgement day.

2

An ark of mercy rode the flood;
  but man, where waters swirled,
rebuilt, impatient of the good,
  another fallen world:
  an unrepentant world.

3

A little child is Adam's heir,
  is Adam's hope and Lord.
Sing joyful carols everywhere
  that Eden is restored:
  in Jesus is restored.

4

Regained is Adam's blessedness:
  the angels sheathe their swords.
In joyful carols all confess⌣
  the kingdom is the Lord's:
  the glory is the Lord's.

F. PRATT GREEN (b. 1903)

The words were written for this tune

192 Rodmell C.M.

English Traditional Melody
adapted by R. Vaughan Williams (1872–1958)

Accept one another as Christ accepted us

When Christ was lifted from the earth
  his hands out-stretched above‿
to every culture, every birth,
  to draw an answering love.

2

Still east and west his love extends,
  and always, near or far,
he calls and claims us as his friends
  and loves us as we are.

3

Thus freely loved, though fully known,
  may I in Christ be free‿
to welcome and accept his own
  as Christ accepted me.

BRIAN A. WREN (b. 1936)
Romans 15.7

193 Offertorium   7 6.7 6.D.   Melody adapted from Michael Haydn
(1737–1806)

Alternative Tune: *Crüger* (A.M.R. 219; E.H. 45; S.P. 87)

The Baptism of Jesus

When Jesus came to Jordan
    to be baptized by John,
he did not come for pardon,
    but as his Father's Son.
He came to share repentance
    with all who mourn their sins,
to speak the vital sentence
    with which good news begins.

2

He came to share temptation,
    our utmost woe and loss;
for us and our salvation
    to die upon the cross.
So when the Dove descended
    on him, the Son of Man,
the hidden years had ended,
    the age of grace began.

3

Come, Holy Spirit, aid us
    to keep the vows we make;
this very day invade us,
    and every bondage break;
come, give our lives direction,
    the gift we covet most –
to share the resurrection
    that leads to Pentecost.

F. PRATT GREEN (b. 1903)

FIRST TUNE

Sheet 8 7.8 7.

Cyril V. Taylor (b. 1907)

SECOND TUNE

Halton Holgate 8 7.8 7.

Later form of tune by
William Boyce (1710–79)

The Nativity of our Lord

Where is this stupendous stranger?
  prophets, shepherds, kings, advise:
lead me to my Master's manger,
  show me where my Saviour lies.

2

O most mighty, O most holy,
  far beyond the seraph's thought,
art thou then so mean and lowly
  as unheeded prophets taught?

3

O the magnitude of meekness,
  worth from worth immortal sprung:
O the strength of infant weakness,
  if eternal is so young.

4

God all-bounteous, all-creative,
  whom no ills from good dissuade,
is incarnate, and a native
  of the very world he made.

CHRISTOPHER SMART (1722–71)

195 Maisemore C.M.   John Dykes Bower (b. 1905)

Alternative Tune: *St. Etheldreda* (A.M.R. 318)

Serving Christ in one another

Where love and loving-kindness dwell,
   there God will ever be:
One Father, Son, and Holy Ghost
   in perfect charity.

2

Brought here together into one
   by Christ our Shepherd-king,
now let us in his love rejoice,
   and of his goodness sing.

3

Here too let God, the living God,
   both loved and honoured be;
and let us each the other love
   with true sincerity.

4

Brought here together by Christ's love,
   let no ill-will divide,
nor quarrels break the unity
   of those for whom he died.

5

Let envy, jealousy and strife
   and all contention cease,
for in our midst serves Christ the Lord,
   our sacrament of peace.

6

Together may we with the saints
   thy face in glory see,
and ever in thy kingdom feast,
   O Christ our God, with thee.

From the Latin Liturgy of Maundy Thursday
tr. GEOFFREY PRESTON (1936–77)

For another translation see no. 132

People of God 7 5.7 5.6 6.6 5.   Patrick Wedd (b. 1948)

Unison

verses 1 and 2   last verse

The People of God

Who are we who stand and sing?
  We are his people.
What this bread and wine we bring?
  Food for his people.
As once with twelve he spake,
poured wine, and bread did break,
  he now will of us make
  a faithful people.

2

What command does he impart
  to us his people?
With your mind and strength and heart
  serve me, my people.
As God in Christ came low,
man's world and work to know,
  to life he bids us go
  to be his people.

3

Who are we who say one creed?
  We are his people.
What the word we hear and read?
  Word for his people.
Through time, in every race,
from earth to farthest space,
  we through our God's good grace
  will be his people.

T. HERBERT O'DRISCOLL (b. 1928)

197 Salzburg C.M.

Melody adapted from Michael Haydn
(1737–1806)

*Christ's compassion
to the weak and tempted*

With joy we meditate the grace
  of our High Priest above;
his heart is made of tenderness,
  and ever yearns with love.

2

Touched with a sympathy within,
  he knows our feeble frame;
he knows what sore temptations mean
  for he has felt the same.

3

He in the days of feeble flesh
  poured out his cries and tears;
and, in his measure, feels afresh
  what every member bears.

4

He'll never quench the smoking flax,
  but raise it to a flame;
the bruisèd reed he never breaks,
  nor scorns the meanest name.

5

Then let our humble faith address
  his mercy and his power:
we shall obtain delivering grace
  in every needful hour.

ISAAC WATTS* (1674–1748)
Hebrews 4. 15–16, and 5. 7

Unison

Harmony (ad lib.)

The Creator

With wonder, Lord, we see your works,
    we see the beauty you have made,
this earth, the skies, all things that are
    in beauty made.

2

With wonder, Lord, we see your works,
    and childlike in our joy we sing
to praise you, bless you, Maker, Lord
    of everything.

3

The stars that fill the skies above,
    the sun and moon which give our light,
are your designing for our use
    and our delight.

4

We praise your works, yet we ourselves
    are works of wonder made by you,
not far from you in all we are
    and all we do.

5

All you have made is ours to rule,
    the birds and beasts at will to tame,
all things to order for the glory
    of your name.

BRIAN FOLEY (b. 1919)
Psalm 8

Lasst uns erfreuen   8 8.4 4.8 8. and Alleluias

Melody from *Geistliche Kirchengesang* (Cologne, 1623)
arr. R. Vaughan Williams (1872–1958)

With angels and archangels

Ye watchers and ye holy ones,
bright Seraphs, Cherubim and Thrones,
   raise the glad strain, Alleluia.
Cry out, Dominions, Princedoms, Powers,
Virtues, Archangels, Angels' choirs,
        Alleluia.

2

O higher than the Cherubim,
more glorious than the Seraphim,
   lead their praises, Alleluia.
Thou Bearer of the eternal Word,
most gracious, magnify the Lord.
        Alleluia.

3

Respond, ye souls in endless rest,
ye Patriarchs and Prophets blest,
   Alleluia, alleluia.
Ye holy Twelve, ye Martyrs strong,
all Saints triumphant, raise the song
        Alleluia.

4

O friends, in gladness let us sing,
supernal anthems echoing,
   Alleluia, alleluia.
To God the Father, God the Son,
and God the Spirit, Three in One,
        Alleluia.

ATHELSTAN RILEY (1858–1945)

200 Palace Green   8 7.8 7.8 8 7.   Michael Fleming (b. 1928)

Christic in glory

You, living Christ, our eyes behold,
   amid your Church appearing,
all girt about your breast with gold
   and bright apparel wearing;
your countenance is burning bright,
a sun resplendent in its might:
   Lord Christ, we see your glory.

2

Your glorious feet have sought and found
   your sons of every nation;
with everlasting voice you sound
   the call of our salvation;
your eyes of flame still search and scan
the whole outspreading realm of man:
   Lord Christ, we see your glory.

3

O risen Christ, today alive,
   amid your Church abiding,
who now your blood and body give,
   new life and strength providing,
we join in heavenly company
to sing your praise triumphantly,
   for we have seen your glory.

E. R. MORGAN (1888–1979)
Revelation 1. 12–16

INDEX OF AUTHORS, TRANSLATORS,
AND SOURCES OF WORDS

INDEX OF COMPOSERS, ARRANGERS, AND SOURCES OF TUNES

* denotes an arrangement

ALPHABETICAL INDEX OF TUNES

METRICAL INDEX OF TUNES

INDEX OF SUBJECTS

INDEX OF FIRST LINES AND TUNES